50 Jubilee (Freedom, Deliverance) truths I learnt from God through my journey to 50

By

Oluwakemi Akinbodewa

"Scriptures are King James Version (KJV) except otherwise stated."

About the Author

Oluwakemi Akinbodewa, was born Oluwakemi Sodiya. She is the second of five children.

After her conversion and graduation from College, she was called into Ministry in 1998.

She served as assistant Pastor to her elder Brother and Mentor. At that time, she was the Women Coordinator, Prayer Leader and Head of Visitation Department.

She became an Enterpreneur in 2002, during her Master's degree.

She was an Assistant Pastor in a church in Maryland, USA.

Because of her passion for business, she has her own Medical Billing Consulting Practice in Maryland, USA and she has contracts with Health Institutions in the United States.

Oluwakemi is married to Christopher, and they both have a Son.

She lives in Maryland, USA and she is currently in the Ministry of discipleship with her Husband.

She was ordained an Evangelist in 1998, and she has been a worker in God's vineyard and an ambassador for Christ everywhere she is.

Dedication

This book is dedicated to my Heavenly Father, who has been both my heavenly and earthly father for 32 years. I give honor to the Almighty God who gives every good and perfect gift.

God is the father of light, and in Him is no variableness, neither shadow of turning. There is no darkness in God at all.

I thank you for giving me light (wisdom, discretion and direction) through your light.

Your constancy, love, integrity and compassion have brought me from where I was to where I am.

I will forever be grateful for your work of salvation and your work of pruning in my life.

You have made me to love who I am and for others to honor who you have made me to be.

I thank you, Lord, for everything!

Isaiah 63:16 "Doubtless thou art our Father, though Abraham be ignorant of us, and Israel acknowledge us not: thou, O LORD, art our Father, our redeemer; thy name is from everlasting."

Acknowledgements:

I would like to appreciate the Almighty God for giving me the life, grace, gift, submission, time, strength and ability to learn from Him and also write this book.

I honor and thank my Friend of 30 years and my Husband of 17 years, Christopher Akinbodewa, for his love, humility, patience, sacrifices and constant support. Your criticism has made me better and your higher expectations from me have yielded results. I thank you for being true and for speaking the truth in love. Your support has added momentum to my life. I will be there with you as you fulfill God's plan and purpose for your life.

I thank God for our son, Michael Akinbodewa, whose conception and birth have brought great favor and prosperity upon my life. You are a reward and a blessing!

I thank God for the father He gave me, Mr. Adebari Sodiya. Your discipline, sacrifices, punctuality, decorum, hard work, generosity, integrity and selflessness are in all of us - your children. I honor you for being a great example to follow. Your sweet memory will never be forgotten.

I can never thank enough, my Mother, Chief (Mrs.) Abiola Sodiya, for her sacrifices and devotion to all her children, and all that God has brought into her life.

You single-handedly raised 5 children after the death of our father 32 years ago, without complaints or compromise.

Your moral excellence is a great example to me and all my siblings. You are truly our Jewel of inestimable value!

I thank God for my older Brother and Mentor, Pastor (Dr.) Mobolaji Sodiya, who is the first member of my immediate birth family to be born again. You saw God's call and gift upon my life, and you gave me the tutoring and opportunity to be established in Ministry. Heaven will reward you for discovering God's gift and grace upon my life.

I would like to appreciate my 3 wonderful and lovely Sisters, Deaconess Mobolanle Bamgbose, Mrs. Olubukola Popoola and Mrs. Aderonke Akinlawon. Thank you for loving me, catering to my needs and for believing in me. The Lord will continually bless you.

My lovely and wonderful Sister, Pastor (Mrs.) Taiwo Sodiya, my lovely Brothers: Mr. Segun Bamgbose, Mr. Segun Popoola and Mr. Akeem Akinlawon, I am humbled by your love, honor and sacrifices for me. You are a blessing to our family!

The contributions of every member of Sodiya to my life is immeasurable. I thank Uncle Zac Shodiya, who has been my father since I relocated to the United States. I will always cherish and honor the memories of Uncle Jacob Shodiya. Mr. Abraham Sodiya, you were there for me in my low estate, and I thank God for preserving you to see who I have become. You all will not lose your rewards.

I thank my new family, Akinbodewa, for accepting me into their family. I appreciate you!

I cannot forget the spiritual contributions of Prophet Francis Aderibigbe, Ado Brethren, The House of Increase and New Bethany WOTCCC to my life. Thank you all for your spiritual support and for believing in me.

I thank Elder Walter and Lady Nicole Thompson III for the opportunity I was given to be their Church's Assistant Pastor for years.

I also thank Minister Henrietta Clements and Bishop Stephanie Stratford for preparing me for ordination as an Elder. The seed you have sown in me will surely bring mighty harvests to the glory of God. I thank you for being faithful in the work of ministry.

To everyone who I did not mention by name, you are not less appreciated. Without you all, I wouldn't have come this far.

I thank you all!

The Lord will continually keep and bless us all. Amen.

Introduction

God's desire is that you become who He has ordained you to be. God wants you to enjoy all things He has given you.

Indeed, God has given you all that you need for life and godliness.

You cannot receive and enjoy all that God has for you without having a relationship with God, knowing and walking in the wisdom of God, self-control, accountability, discretion, working and partnering with God to fulfill His plan for your life. You cannot be who God wants you to be and have what God wants you to have without knowing how to have healthy and successful relationships, and a prosperous purpose.

God wants you to have it all. God delights in your all-around prosperity.

The Lord puts it in my heart to share with you how He made me to be all-around successful by teaching me these freedom truths.

I believe God will do the same for you as you submit yourself to the tutoring and leading of the Holy Spirit as you read this book.

I believe God for a better and an unbelievable NEW YOU that will make people to be confused if it's you.

Jesus did it for the man who was born blind in the Bible, and He wants to do the same for you (John 9:8-9).

For you to have a transformed life, you need to have a personal relationship with God by confessing and repenting of your sins, and accepting Jesus as your Lord and Savior.

You need to believe God has a purpose for you.

Discover it and begin to fulfill God's purpose for your life!

Scriptural Foundation:

John 8:31-32 "Then said Jesus to those Jews which believed on him, If ye continue in my word, then are ye my disciples indeed; and ye shall know the truth, and the truth shall make you free."

2 Timothy 1:13 "You have heard me tell you about God's true message. Let those words be an example to you so that you also teach what is true. Do this because you belong to Christ Jesus. Continue to trust him and to love his people." EASY

2 Timothy 3:10-11 "But you, Timothy, certainly know what I teach, and how I live, and what my purpose in life is. You know my faith, my patience, my love, and my endurance. You know how much persecution and suffering I have endured. You know all about how I was persecuted in Antioch, Iconium, and Lystra—but the Lord rescued me from all of it." NLT

Galatians 5:1 "It is for freedom that Christ has set us free. Stand firm, then, and do not let yourselves be burdened again by a yoke of slavery." NIV

Romans 8:1-2 "There is therefore now no condemnation to them which are in Christ Jesus, who walk not after the flesh, but after the Spirit. For the law of the Spirit of life in Christ Jesus hath made me free from the law of sin and death."

John 17:17 "Sanctify them through thy truth: thy word is truth."

Ephesians 4:13-15 "This will continue until we all come to such unity in our faith and knowledge of God's Son that we will be mature in the Lord, measuring up to the full and complete standard of Christ. Then we will no longer be immature like children. We won't be tossed and blown about by every wind of new teaching. We will not be influenced when people try to trick us with lies so clever they sound like the truth. "Instead, we will speak the truth in love, growing in every way more and more like Christ, who is the head of his body, the church."" NLT

Leviticus 25:10 "And ye shall hallow the fiftieth year, and proclaim liberty throughout all the land unto all the inhabitants thereof: it shall be a jubile unto you; and ye shall return every man unto his possession, and ye shall return every man unto his family."

Proverbs 30:5 "All of God's word has proven to be true. He is a shield to those who come to him for protection." GW

John 14:6 "Jesus saith unto him, I am the way, the truth, and the life: no man cometh unto the Father, but by me."

Table of Contents

THE SPIRITUAL CONTROLS THE PHYSICAL

If you don't breakthrough in the spirit through communion with God, the study of God's Word, faith in and confession of God's Word, prayers, and fasting, you can't breakthrough in the physical.

Apostle Paul said an open door was opened to him, but there were many adversaries.

There are always spiritual adversaries that manifest through physical adversaries against God's will and purpose for your life.

This is why the Bible says that we fight against principalities and powers and rulers of darkness.

Don't be naive! You are engaging in a spiritual battle against your breakthroughs and God's purpose for your life.

Fight with the spiritual weapons of the blood of Jesus, the name of Jesus, the Word of God, and the Worship of God. Yes, praise is a weapon against the onslaught of the enemy and his spiritual and physical agents.

You must be born again to become God's child and be in Christ so that you can have access to heavenly blessings through Jesus Christ.

Ephesians 1:3 "All praise to God, the Father of our Lord Jesus Christ, who has blessed us with every spiritual blessing in the heavenly realms because we are united with Christ." NLT

Daniel 10:12-14 "Then he said, "Don't be afraid, Daniel. Since the first day you began to pray for understanding and to humble yourself before your God, your request has been heard in heaven. I have come in answer to your prayer. But for twenty-one days, the spirit prince of the kingdom of Persia blocked my way. Then Michael, one of the archangels, came to help me, and I left him there with the spirit prince of the kingdom of Persia. Now I am here to explain what will happen to your people in the future, for this vision concerns a time yet to come."" NLT

Ephesians 6:11-13, 16-18 "Put on the whole armour of God, that ye may be able to stand against the wiles of the devil. For we wrestle not against flesh and blood, but against principalities, against powers, against the rulers of the darkness of this world, against spiritual wickedness in high places. Wherefore take unto you the whole armour of God, that ye may be able to withstand in the evil day, and having done all, to stand; above all, taking the shield of faith, wherewith ye shall be able to quench all the fiery darts of the wicked. And take the helmet of salvation, and the sword of the Spirit, which is the word of God: praying always with all prayer and supplication in the Spirit, and watching thereunto with all perseverance and supplication for all saints."

THERE IS A SCRIPT THAT WAS WRITTEN ABOUT YOU AND EVERYONE BEFORE BIRTH

Your success, joy, and peace are in discovering and living according to that script and your purpose.

Doing what others are doing will make you confused and frustrated.

God created you for a purpose. All that you are, all that you have, and the path you have taken in life, are purposefully for the fulfillment of God's will and plan for your life.

You were born into your family and community for a purpose.

You are living out the prophecies and preordained plan for your life.

God knew you before you were formed in your mother's belly. God knew you before your parents came together.

God called you for a purpose before you were born, and He endowed you with all that you need to be who He has called you to be.

Discover your script in the Scriptures and by your gifting, and you will discover and fulfill God's will for your life.

When you fulfill God's purpose for your life, you have fulfillment.

Hebrews 10:7 "Then said I, Lo, I come (In the volume of the book it is written of me) To do thy will, O God."

John 18:37 ""Pilate asked him, So you are a king?" Jesus replied, "You're correct in saying that I'm a king. I have been born and have come into the world for this reason: to testify to the truth. Everyone who belongs to the truth listens to me."" GW

Jeremiah 1:4-7, 9-10 "Then the word of the LORD came unto me, saying, Before I formed thee in the belly I knew thee; and before thou camest forth out of the womb I sanctified thee, and I ordained thee a prophet unto the nations. Then said I, Ah, Lord GOD! behold, I cannot speak: for I am a child. But the LORD said unto me, Say not, I am a child: for thou shalt go to all that I shall send thee, and whatsoever I command thee thou shalt speak. Then the LORD put forth his hand and touched my mouth. And the LORD said unto me, Behold, I have put my words in thy mouth. See, I have this day set thee over the nations and over the kingdoms, to root out, and to pull down, and to destroy, and to throw down, to build, and to plant."

A BORROWER IS A SERVANT OF THE LENDER

Knowing this made me pray for and live a debt-free life.

Financial Freedom is needed to be who God wants you to be and not to live a life of compromise.

Don't live above your means.

Be self-controlled. Be self-disciplined. Don't buy things because others are buying them.

Stay away from friends who make you buy things on impulse. Have accountability friends who you go over your expensive purchases with before you buy them. Submit yourself to them and their scrutiny.

Ask yourself some questions before you make expensive purchases.

Do I need this product at this time?

Can I afford to buy this product at this time?

Can I do without this purchase?

What value will this purchase add to me?

Does my current state of life or season of life require or accommodate this purchase?

Will the value of this purchase increase or decrease over time?

Can I return or sell this purchase if I don't need it anymore?

Will this purchase be a blessing or burden to my children after I'm dead?

Does this purchase affect my/our savings?

Will my spouse agree to this purchase, or will it bring a disagreement between us later on?

These are some questions you can ask yourself or allow others to ask you.

Be truthful in your answers to these questions, and this will help you to make the right decisions about your spending.

God has given you the spirit of self-control; walk in it.

Make a commitment not to leave debt for your family to settle. Pray against whatsoever will make you live and die in debt.

Be a blessing and not a burden.

Proverbs 22:7 "A rich person rules poor people, and a borrower is a slave to a lender." GW

2 Kings 4:1 "Now there cried a certain woman of the wives of the sons of the prophets unto Elisha, saying, Thy servant my husband is dead; and thou knowest that thy servant did fear the LORD: and the creditor is come to take unto him my two sons to be bondmen."

SOLITARY IS NEEDED TO PREPARE AND TO BE WHO GOD WANTS YOU TO BE

Jesus always left the crowd to a solitary place to pray and be refreshed.

Don't be running around for a platform. If God does not establish or help you, nobody can establish or help you.

God is the lifter of every head. Don't come out before your time. Don't rush your preparation process.

Spend time in prayer and preparation. You need the power and presence of God to be relevant.

As a child of God, know that God can only use you and bless you when you have gone through the refiner's fire and His school of discipline, suffering, temperance, patience, and long-suffering, which have resulted in your total and absolute dependence on Him.

When you are successful in this training, nothing matters anymore but God and His Word.

At the right time, the Lord will publicly announce you.

Galatians 1:15-18 "But even before I was born, God chose me and called me by his marvelous grace. Then it pleased him to reveal his Son to me so that I would proclaim the Good News about Jesus to the Gentiles. When this happened, I did not rush out to consult with any human being. Nor did I go up to Jerusalem to consult with those who were apostles before I was. Instead, I went away into Arabia, and later I returned to the city of Damascus. Then three years later, I went to Jerusalem to get to know Peter, and I stayed with him for fifteen days."

1 Samuel 3:19-20 "And Samuel grew, and the LORD was with him, and did let none of his words fall to the ground. And all Israel from Dan even to Beer-sheba knew that Samuel was established to be a prophet of the LORD."

FAITH IS REQUIRED FOR YOU TO HAVE IN THE PHYSICAL WHAT YOU WERE GIVEN AND PROMISED IN THE SPIRIT

Have faith in God that you will be and have what God has promised you.

Don't have alternatives or help God to fulfill His will and purpose for your life.

Wait patiently on the Lord and follow the examples of those who received from the Lord through faith and patience.

When the Lord gives a vision or a purpose, the expectation is that the Lord will fulfill it immediately.

But what happens is that, when God gives a Word, the kingdom of darkness unleashes an opposition to the fulfillment of God's Word.

God allows the opposition of the devil, to show forth His glory, His power and His supremacy (Romans 9:17).

When Jesus was born, Herod raised an opposition by trying to kill Jesus (Matthew 2:13).

When it was God's appointed time for Jesus to die and shed His blood for the remission of the sins of man, the devil did not want Jesus to die, so that God's purpose for sending Christ to the earth and redeeming man will not be fulfilled.

Jesus' purpose was to die and reconcile man to God through the shedding of His blood, but the devil did not want this to happen (Matthew 16:21–23).

Jesus' coming was to destroy the works of the devil, and deliver man from the kingdom of the devil to the Kingdom of God (1 John 3:8b, Colossians 1:13).

When God raised Paul to become an Apostle to the Gentiles, the devil tried severally to kill Paul through the Jews (Acts 23:12).

An opposition to God's Word or God's revealed vision or purpose means that you are in the will of God. God will surely give you the victory, and fulfill His purpose and vision for your life, if you don't lose your faith.

Remind yourself always that God's purpose cannot be stopped (Job 42:2).

Your faith will stand based on your knowledge of God and confidence in God. Those who know their God shall do exploits (Daniel 11:32b).

You should be confident in God's power to deliver you and your purpose from the opposition of the devil, and His faithfulness to fulfill at the appointed time, His Word, purpose and the vision that He has given to you.

Have an absolute faith in God, that your purpose will be fulfilled according to what He has told you or shown you (Acts 27:25).

The Lord does not just stand by you in the battle against your faith and purpose, the Lord goes before you to fight and win your battles; as you trust and obey His instructions (Judges 4:14–16).

YOU ARE NEVER ALONE AND WITHOUT GOD'S HELP (Matthew 28:20).

The Lord always does exceedingly, abundantly and above what you ask or think, according to His power that works in you. Let your faith be great, so that you can be able to fulfill all that God has ordained for you to do, by the power of the Holy Spirit.

You should not let delay, storms from the devil, and challenges of life steal away the faith and hope that you have in God and His plan for your life.

Despite the fight against your faith, you should never forget God's faithfulness to fulfill His plan and purpose for you and through you.

Walk in the boldness of the Holy Spirit and do all that God would have you do.

Have absolute faith in God to fulfill at the appointed time, what He has told you and called you to do.

Obey God in the midst of the fight against your faith, and you will see the salvation of the Lord.

He/she who believes does not make haste. Stay away from friends who feed your hastiness or desire to walk in the flesh or doubt God.

God's promise is sure, have faith that it will be exactly as God has said it will be.

God is not a man that He should lie. He is not a son of man, that He should repent of His promises to you.

Study God's Word. Stand upon God's Word. Faith comes by hearing God's Word.

Also, speak and act consistently with your faith. Don't believe one thing and say another thing. Make sure your words and actions are in line with your faith in God, His Word, and promises for you.

It shall be for you, as God had said it will be!

Luke 1:45 "And blessed is she that believed: for there shall be a performance of those things which were told her from the Lord."

Acts 27:25 "Wherefore, sirs, be of good cheer: for I believe God, that it shall be even as it was told me."

1 John 5:4–5 "For whatsoever is born of God overcometh the world: and this is the victory that overcometh the world,

even our faith. Who is he that overcometh the world, but he that believeth that Jesus is the Son of God?"

1 Corinthians 15:57-58 "But thanks be to God, which giveth us the victory through our Lord Jesus Christ. Therefore, my beloved brethren, be ye stedfast, unmoveable, always abounding in the work of the Lord, forasmuch as ye know that your labour is not in vain in the Lord."

IN THE MULTITUDE OF COUNSELORS, THERE IS SAFETY

Everyone has a blind spot.

You may not see all the sides of and to a thing.

Have 2 or 3 trusted, experienced, and spiritually mature people who you review your plans with before you make a major decision.

Listen to the concerns of your advisers and look into them judiciously.

Your answers to their questions may make you see some red flags that you previously ignored or did not see.

Your final decision must align with God's Word and God's revealed will for your life.

Proverbs 11:14 "Where no counsel is, the people fall: But in the multitude of counsellors there is safety."

Proverbs 15:22 "Plans go wrong for lack of advice; many advisers bring success." NLT

DISCRETION IS REQUIRED TO HAVE A PEACEABLE AND STRESS-FREE LIFE

Discretion comes from the wisdom of God. That is why Apostle James said in James 1:5, "If anyone lacks wisdom, he should ask of God."

When I say the right thing at the wrong time or to the wrong people, I feel a conviction of the Holy Spirit.

A life of total submission to the Holy Spirit will help you to live a life of discretion.

Discretion will give you long life and preserve your prosperity.

Discretion will keep you away from false friends and save you from fraudsters.

Choose your friends and those who have access to your life and influence your decisions with discretion.

Lack of discretion will make your dreams known and revealed prematurely, and this may bring stolen, aborted, and hijacked dreams and plans.

Discretion is saying or doing the right thing at the right time, in the right place, with the right people, and according to God's will.

1 Samuel 10:14-16 "And Saul's uncle said unto him and to his servant, Whither went ye? And he said, To seek the

asses: and when we saw that they were nowhere, we came to Samuel. And Saul's uncle said, Tell me, I pray thee, what Samuel said unto you. And Saul said unto his uncle, He told us plainly that the asses were found. But of the matter of the kingdom, whereof Samuel spake, he told him not."

Nehemiah 2:12 "And I arose in the night, I and some few men with me; neither told I any man what my God had put in my heart to do at Jerusalem: neither was there any beast with me, save the beast that I rode upon."

1 Samuel 9:27 "When they reached the edge of town, Samuel told Saul to send his servant on ahead. After the servant was gone, Samuel said, "Stay here, for I have received a special message for you from God."" NLT

SECULAR AND SPIRITUAL EDUCATION ARE VERY IMPORTANT

Be a student or graduate of a discipline or skill and a student of the Word.

Ignorance will not make you academically, spiritually, financially, mentally, emotionally, and physically free.

Keep learning and imparting knowledge as long as you live.

The greatest inheritance you can give your children is knowledge, not money.

Knowledge will make them preserve and multiply the riches that you have given them.

You cannot be who God wants you to be and have what God wants you to have if you despise knowledge.

John 8:31-32 "Then said Jesus to those Jews which believed on him, If ye continue in my word, then are ye my disciples indeed; and ye shall know the truth, and the truth shall make you free."

Hosea 4:6 "my people are destroyed from lack of knowledge. "Because you have rejected knowledge, I also reject you as my priests; because you have ignored the law of your God, I also will ignore your children."" NIV

2 Timothy 2:15 "Study to shew thyself approved unto God, a workman that needeth not to be ashamed, rightly dividing the word of truth."

HONOR AND PROTECT YOUR FAMILY

Your honor, sacrifices, and service to your immediate family should be next to your submission, love, and relationship with God.

Never put commitments to church, ministry, work, or business above your family.

Never put any human above or before your Husband or Wife. Doing this causes disorder and confusion in the family, which ultimately leads to problems in the house, separation, or divorce.

The due order is the husband, wife, and child/children.

As much as you can, do not let anyone raise, advise or control your child or children in their formative years without your permission and approval.

Ephesians 5:22-23 "Wives, submit yourselves unto your own husbands, as unto the Lord. For the husband is the head of the wife, even as Christ is the head of the church: and he is the saviour of the body."

1 Peter 3:7 "In the same way, you husbands must give honor to your wives. Treat your wife with understanding as you live together. She may be weaker than you are, but she is your equal partner in God's gift of new life. Treat her as you should so your prayers will not be hindered." NLT

1 Timothy 5:8 "If anyone doesn't take care of his own relatives, especially his immediate family, he has denied the Christian faith and is worse than an unbeliever." GW

GIVING DELIVERS FROM GREED

Giving delivers you from worshipping and idolizing yourself.

Giving delivers you from living for yourself.

You have a larger purpose that is more than yourself.

There are many destinies that are connected to your giving, and your destiny is connected to another person's giving.

Your life does not consist of what you have.

Have a percentage of your income that you give to your family and others regularly.

Giving is saving, though this contradicts academic financial principles.

When you give, you give God the opportunity to make others give to you.

God's principles have been tried and tested, and they work everywhere and in every season of life.

Proverbs 11:24-25 "Give freely and become more wealthy; be stingy and lose everything. The generous will prosper; those who refresh others will themselves be refreshed." NLT

Proverbs 19:17 "If you help the poor, you are lending to the Lord— and he will repay you." NLT

Luke 6:38 "give, and it shall be given unto you; good measure, pressed down, and shaken together, and running over, shall men give into your bosom. For with the same measure that ye mete withal it shall be measured to you again."

1 Timothy 6:17-19 "Teach those who are rich in this world not to be proud and not to trust in their money, which is so unreliable. Their trust should be in God, who richly gives us all we need for our enjoyment. Tell them to use their money to do good. They should be rich in good works and generous to those in need, always being ready to share with others. By doing this, they will be storing up their treasure as a good foundation for the future so that they may experience true life." NLT

HONOR YOUR FATHER AND YOUR MOTHER

Your longevity and all-around well-being are dependent on honoring your father and mother.

Give regularly to your parents and be involved in their physical, spiritual, financial, and emotional well-being.

God made children to be a reward and a blessing to their parents.

Every child must know this and be a blessing to their parents.

Have your parent(s) care expenses in your monthly budget, as much as you can.

If one parent or both are dead, fulfill their dream(s) that is/are according to God's will for you to do or continue giving to the Organization (Spiritual and/or Non-spiritual) they partnered with as much as you can and for how long you can.

Honoring your parents preserves and elongates your life and makes you receive blessings from God and your earthly parents.

Ephesians 6:1-3 "Children, obey your parents because you belong to the Lord, for this is the right thing to do. "Honor your father and mother." This is the first commandment with a promise: If you honor your father and mother, "things will go well for you, and you will have a long life on the earth.""

Proverbs 23:22 "Listen to your father, who gave you life, and don't despise your mother when she is old."

BE DILIGENT IN WHAT YOU DO

Without diligence, the breakthrough that you prayed and fasted for will not materialize or last.

I am highly experienced, diligent, and constantly learning and improving in all that I do.

Greatness requires you to be diligent continually.

God's Word, will, and promise for your life cannot be actualized without you being diligent in what God has called you to do.

God is a worker, and He requires all His children to be workers, too.

Jesus is working right now by making intercessions for the saints.

The Holy Spirit is working on earth to fulfill the Will and Purpose of God everywhere and in the lives of the saints.

Why don't you start working diligently from today so you can be like your Heavenly Father and also experience the manifestation of God's Word and Will for you?

John 5:17 "But Jesus replied, "My Father is always working, and so am I."" NLT

Proverbs 22:29 "Do you see a man diligent and skillful in his business? He will stand before kings; he will not stand before obscure men." AMPC

Proverbs 12:24 "The hand of the diligent will rule, but the slothful will be put to forced labor." AMPC

YOUR DRESSING MATTERS

If Jesus' garment was not exquisite, they would not have cast lots for His garment.

God constantly leads me to where to buy fabulous dresses at affordable prices. Believe God to do the same and much more for you.

Be intentional in your dressing.

Take time to plan and prepare how to dress for every outing.

Also, dress modestly, virtuously, and appropriately at all times because you never know what God will do through you and for you at any time.

You may not have the opportunity to go and change your clothes when God introduces you to the world or would have you represent Him.

Matthew 27:35 "And they crucified him, and parted his garments, casting lots: that it might be fulfilled which was spoken by the prophet, They parted my garments among them, and upon my vesture did they cast lots."

Ecclesiastes 9:8 "Put on nice clothes and make yourself look good." NCV

AS MANY AS ARE LED BY THE SPIRIT OF GOD ARE THE SONS OF GOD

Obedience to God is key to your sonship. Jesus is your Lord when you obey Him.

I live to know God's will and to obey His will and purpose for my life at all times.

Seek to know and live by God's Word and will for your life as revealed by the Holy Spirit.

Disobedience to God's revealed will is costly, and it can lead to struggles, fruitless efforts, physical and spiritual death.

Your all-around prosperity is in your obedience to God, His Word, and His revealed will for your life.

God wants you to obey Him and His Word more than any sacrifice of worship or sacrifice of giving.

The question that comes to mind is why does God want your obedience?

Obedience to God shows and proves that you trust God and believe in Him and His Word more than anyone or anything.

Obedience to God, His will and Word expresses your faith in God's wisdom and judgment.

Obedience to God's commandment gives you hope in a future blessing of eternal life.

Your obedience to God and His Word serves as a witness to God and the authenticity of the gospel.

God wants you to obey Him because He has done great and mighty things for you that should make you to honor and obey Him.

Also, God knows that your blessings are in your obedience to Him and His commandments.

The blessings of obedience to God include long life, supernatural supply, abundance, open heavens, refreshing, increase, satisfaction, protection and prosperity.

More importantly, God wants you to obey Him and to teach your children to obey Him because of your generational perpetuation.

Your love for God should cause you to obey Him.

Obey God because He loves you and you love Him, too.

Deuteronomy 28:1-2, 6 "And it shall come to pass, if thou shalt hearken diligently unto the voice of the LORD thy God, to observe and to do all his commandments which I command thee this day, that the LORD thy God will set thee on high above all nations of the earth: and all these blessings shall come on thee, and overtake thee if thou shalt hearken unto the voice of the LORD thy God. Blessed shalt thou be when thou comest in, and blessed shalt thou be when thou goest out."

Luke 6:46 "And why call ye me, Lord, Lord, and do not the things which I say?"

John 2:5 "His mother saith unto the servants, Whatsoever he saith unto you, do it."

Romans 8:14 "For as many as are led by the Spirit of God, they are the sons of God."

ENJOY YOUR FAMILY NOW

Enjoy your family and spend time with them as you work, do business, and ministry.

Structure all you do around your family.

Don't wait till you retire before you spend time with your family.

Your family will not be in the same place and state they are right now when you retire.

Put your family before any work, business, or ministry.

Teach your children the Way and Word of God when they are young.

Doing this will save you from stress when you are old.

As much as possible, involve your family in all or most things that you do.

Let their input and voice matter to you. Seek their opinion on how the family can spend fulfilling time together.

Proverbs 5:18-19 "Let your own fountain be blessed, and enjoy the girl you married when you were young, a loving doe and a graceful deer. Always let her breasts satisfy you. Always be intoxicated with her love." GW

Ephesians 6:4 "Fathers, do not make your children angry, but raise them with the training and teaching of the Lord." NCV

Titus 2:4-5 "that they may teach the young women to be sober, to love their husbands, to love their children, to be discreet, chaste, keepers at home, good, obedient to their own husbands, that the word of God be not blasphemed."

BE HONEST

Honesty might not pay fast, but it pays longer than dishonesty.

Be honest and faithful in all that you do and in your relationships with others.

Honesty makes you to be reliable and trusted.

It makes you to be retained at work and have a successful ministry and/or business.

Honesty will make your ministry and business continue to exist.

Honesty does not only bring money and success, but it also secures your eternal life, and it brings peace and joy.

Be clear and truthful in all your dealings. If anything changes make it known beforehand. Let your weight or measure be just as instructed by God.

Know that you are Christ's representative in all things and at all times. Represent Christ the best way you can!

2 Corinthians 8:21 "providing for honest things, not only in the sight of the Lord but also in the sight of men."

Deuteronomy 25:15 "But thou shalt have a perfect and just weight, a perfect and just measure shalt thou have: that thy days may be lengthened in the land which the LORD thy God giveth thee."

Revelation 21:8 "But the fearful, and unbelieving, and the abominable, and murderers, and whoremongers, and sorcerers, and idolaters, and all liars, shall have their part in the lake which burneth with fire and brimstone: which is the second death."

BE PUNCTUAL AT ALL TIMES

If God is late in anything, catastrophic situations will arise.

Your lateness is grave, and it affects someone or something.

Prepare ahead to be early for every engagement.

Punctuality is proof of your faithfulness.

If you can't be punctual to an event due to unforeseen circumstance(s), communicate to the applicable authority as soon as you can.

This gives time for a replacement for any role you were assigned to fulfill. If you are not a participant in the event, still plan to be punctual.

What if you were in charge or a participant in an event, and only you came on time?

Be punctual at any event you plan to attend, as much as you can.

Your punctuality matters and it will be noticed and greatly rewarded by God and man.

1 Corinthians 4:2 "Moreover, it is required in stewards that a man be found faithful."

1 Corinthians 14:40 "Let all things be done decently and in order."

Ecclesiastes 3:1 "To everything there is a season and a time to every purpose under the heaven."

DO TO OTHERS WHAT YOU WANT THEM TO DO TO YOU

Be mindful of how you treat and speak to and about other people.

God created every soul and cares for and about every soul.

God sees and cares about how you treat other people.

Maltreating others has grave consequences from both God and man.

Whatever you do to others has a way of coming back to you.

Don't speak to others the way you don't want to be spoken to.

Don't ridicule or belittle others. You surely don't want anyone to do the same to you. Think over your words and choose your words before you speak, especially when you are angry.

People may forget the scenario, but they will not forget the hurtful words that you said.

Hurtful words are cancer that eats deep. Do not make people bitter and broken; make them better and whole.

Speak words of encouragement to others and build others up with your words. God will raise other people to encourage you and build you up, too.

Always think about how you will feel if what you are about to say or do, was done to you before you say or do the same to others.

Luke 6:31 "Do to others as you would like them to do to you."

Genesis 44:16 "And Judah said, What shall we say to my Lord? What shall we reply? Or how shall we clear ourselves, since God has found out and exposed the iniquity of your servants? Behold, we are my Lord's slaves, the rest of us as well as he with whom the cup is found." AMPC

YOU REAP WHAT YOU SOW

Support others, and God will raise support for you.

Sow peace, and you will reap peace.

Sow honor, and you will reap honor.

Sow love, and you will reap love.

Sow prayers for others, and you will reap prayers from others.

Keep other people's secrets so that your secrets can be kept, too.

Sow generously, and you will reap generously. Sow good seeds so you can reap mighty harvests during your lifetime, and your children will continue to reap the harvests of seeds you have sown, after your lifetime.

If you are not reaping the good that you are sowing; fast, pray, and believe God for deliverance from whatsoever is hindering your harvest.

If you sow into your spirit (by being born again, studying the Word of God, praying and fasting, listening to Scriptural-based messages, and living by God's Word), you will reap everlasting life.

Genesis 8:22 "While the earth remaineth, seedtime and harvest, and cold and heat, and summer and winter, and day and night shall not cease."

Matthew 13:24-25, 28b "Another parable put he forth unto them, saying, The kingdom of heaven is likened unto a man which sowed good seed in his field: but while men slept, his enemy came and sowed tares among the wheat, and went his way. He said unto them, An enemy hath done this."

Galatians 6:7-8 "Be not deceived; God is not mocked: for whatsoever a man soweth, that shall he also reap. For he that soweth to his flesh shall of the flesh reap corruption; but he that soweth to the Spirit shall of the Spirit reap life everlasting."

2 Samuel 9:1–7 "And David said, Is there yet any that is left of the house of Saul, that I may shew him kindness for Jonathan's sake? And there was of the house of Saul a servant whose name was Ziba. And when they had called him unto David, the king said unto him, Art thou Ziba? And he said, Thy servant is he. And the king said, Is there not yet any of the house of Saul, that I may shew the kindness of God unto him? And Ziba said unto the king, Jonathan hath yet a son, which is lame on his feet. And the king said unto him, Where is he? And Ziba said unto the king, Behold, he is in the house of Machir, the son of Ammiel, in Lodebar. Then king David sent, and fetched him out of the house of Machir, the son of Ammiel, from Lodebar. Now when Mephibosheth, the son of Jonathan, the son of Saul, was

come unto David, he fell on his face, and did reverence. And David said, Mephibosheth. And he answered, Behold, thy servant! And David said unto him, Fear not: for I will surely shew thee kindness for Jonathan thy father's sake, and will restore thee all the land of Saul, thy father; and thou shalt eat bread at my table continually."

MIND WHAT YOU THINK

You are what you think.

You can never be greater than your thoughts.

A wrong mindset will hinder your believing and possessing all that God has in store for you.

Think about this: What if God does what I'm thinking? Will it be something good or bad?

As a believer, you have the mind of Christ, and you have the ability to think like Christ.

Cast down every lie of the enemy and grasshopper mentality, and make them obedient to what God says about you. Always say God's Word over your life.

I am the head and not the tail.

I can do all things through Christ who strengthens me.

God has given me all that pertains to life and godliness.

The Lord will supply all my needs according to His riches in glory.

I am seated in heavenly places with Christ. I am a royal priesthood.

As for me and my house, we will serve the Lord.

My children shall be taught of the Lord, and great shall be their peace.

I am a good thing, and my husband/wife shall obtain favor from the Lord.

Look up God's promises about you in the Bible and confess them at all times.

God will do exceedingly, abundantly, and above what you think; therefore, think great things that are in line with God's will and purpose for your life.

What you watch or see, read, hear, and are exposed to will influence your mind and thoughts.

If you need healing because of a broken heart, pray to God to heal you and make you whole, so you can think as He thinks.

Mind what you think because you will eventually confess and act what you think.

Philippians 4:8 "Finally, brethren, whatsoever things are true, whatsoever things are honest, whatsoever things are just, whatsoever things are pure, whatsoever things are lovely, whatsoever things are of good report; if there be any virtue, and if there be any praise, think on these things."

Proverbs 23:7b "For as he thinks in his heart, so is he."

Romans 12:2 "And be not conformed to this world: but be ye transformed by the renewing of your mind, that ye may prove what is that good, and acceptable, and perfect, will of God."

MIND WHAT YOU CONFESS

Words are powerful.

Death and life are in the power of the tongue.

You have what you confess.

You become what you confess.

Pray for deliverance from evil or wrong confession.

You cannot confess God's Word and promise if you don't study God's Word.

Read and meditate on God's Word daily.

Confess the Word of the Lord until it's engraved in your heart.

Stand upon God's Word and believe God's Word will grow mightily on your behalf and prevail over every challenge that you are going through.

Numbers 14:28 "Say unto them, As truly as I live, saith the LORD, as ye have spoken in mine ears, so will I do to you."

Joshua 1:8 "This book of the law shall not depart out of thy mouth; but thou shalt meditate therein day and night, that thou mayest observe to do according to all that is written therein: for then thou shalt make thy way prosperous, and then thou shalt have good success."

LET GO OF YOUR PAST!

No matter how hard you hold on to the past, it's in the past, it's gone, and it will hinder you from entering your glorious future.

Confess your sins, repent, and believe God has forgiven you.

Ask for forgiveness from those who you have hurt, and pray to God to touch their hearts to forgive you and bless you.

Do not let your past determine your future.

God has given you an opportunity to begin again.

Begin to walk in the fullness of who God has called you to be by receiving and enjoying a fresh start.

Do all that you can, with the help of the Holy Spirit, to make changes in your life and stick to it.

You can't continue in sin and expect the grace of God to abound.

You can't continue to spend money recklessly and expect your finances to be in order.

You can't continue to be lazy and expect great things to happen in your life.

You can't continue to be ignorant and expect to be a leader or a professional.

Be the best that you can, and your unhealthy past will fade away.

Let people begin to ask themselves if this is you because of the transformation that has taken place in your life.

Make headlines and let the new YOU become unbelievable to critics like the man who was born blind in John 9:1-38.

Receive and enjoy new mercies from God that will usher you into your glorious future.

2 Corinthians 5:17 "Therefore, if any man be in Christ, he is a new creature: old things are passed away; behold, all things are become new."

Judges 17:1-2 "And there was a man of mount Ephraim, whose name was Micah. And he said unto his mother, The eleven hundred shekels of silver that were taken from thee, about which thou cursedst, and spakest of also in mine ears, behold, the silver is with me; I took it. And his mother said, Blessed be thou of the LORD, my son."

John 9:6–9 "Then he spit on the ground, made mud with the saliva, and spread the mud over the blind man's eyes. He told him, "Go wash yourself in the pool of Siloam" (Siloam means "sent"). So the man went and washed and came back seeing! His neighbors and others who knew him as a blind beggar asked each other, "Isn't this the man who used to sit and beg?" Some said he was, and others said, "No, he just looks like him!" But the beggar kept saying, "Yes, I am the same one!"" NLT

SAVE MONEY

Save money for tomorrow.

God's daily provision does not exempt believers from saving.

Joseph advised Pharaoh to save for the coming famine.

God wants you to be wise and spend your money and use everything that He has given you wisely.

Save money so that you buy expensive purchases with cash, and you don't have to pay interest.

Save money so that you can give some of it to the poor and less privileged.

Save so that you can be a financial partner to ministries and churches that are doing God's work.

Save so that you can leave an inheritance to your children and grandchildren.

God has blessed you to be a blessing.

Save so that you can be the blessing you are.

God can discipline you if you don't spend your money judiciously.

Some of the dealings of God could be a lack of favor and blessings from God and man.

Luke 15:11-16 "And he said, A certain man had two sons: and the younger of them said to his father, Father, give me the portion of goods that falleth to me. And he divided unto them his living. And not many days after the younger son gathered all together and took his journey into a far country, and there wasted his substance with riotous living. And when he had spent all, there arose a mighty famine in that land; and he began to be in want. And he went and joined himself to a citizen of that country; and he sent him into his fields to feed swine. And he would fain have filled his belly with the husks that the swine did eat: and no man gave unto him."

Genesis 41:34-36 "Make arrangements to appoint supervisors over the land to take a fifth of Egypt's harvest during the seven good years. Have them collect all the food during these good years and store up grain under Pharaoh's control, to be kept for food in the cities. This food will be a reserve supply for our country during the seven years of famine that will happen in Egypt. Then the land will not be ruined by the famine."

Hebrews 12:5–6 "You have forgotten the encouraging words that God speaks to you as his children: "My child, pay attention when the Lord disciplines you. Don't give up when he corrects you. The Lord disciplines everyone he loves. He severely disciplines everyone he accepts as his child.""
GW

YOU ARE A SPIRIT, YOU HAVE A SOUL, BUT YOU LIVE IN A BODY

Prepare your body for your old age in your young age.

Take care of your body.

Pray for sound health because you cannot function if you are not healthy.

Bathe regularly. Clean your house, your clothes, and everything your body lives in.

Germs breathe in dirty environments and will make you sick.

Stay away from stressful situations because one of the causes of sickness is stress.

The Lord wants you to live a stress-free life.

The Lord has given you the power to overcome every situation and life challenge through His Word.

God gave doctors and other medical professionals to advise and treat medically.

Pray for your healing and seek medical help if required.

Do not seek medical help before you pray for your healing. God is against doing this.

God is not against medications; God can use medications and anything He wants to perfect your health and all that concerns you. If you must go through surgery, believe that God will make the surgery or procedure to work for your good.

Don't be ashamed if you have to take medications or undergo surgery as a believer. God works all things together for our good.

2 Chronicles 16:12 "And Asa in the thirty and ninth year of his reign was diseased in his feet until his disease was exceeding great: yet in his disease, he sought not to the LORD, but to the physicians."

3 John 1:2 "Beloved, I wish above all things that thou mayest prosper and be in health, even as thy soul prospereth."

1 Timothy 5:23 "Don't drink only water. You ought to drink a little wine for the sake of your stomach because you are sick so often." NLT

Exodus 15:26 "and said, If thou wilt diligently hearken to the voice of the LORD thy God, and wilt do that which is right in his sight, and wilt give ear to his commandments, and keep all his statutes, I will put none of these diseases upon thee, which I have brought upon the Egyptians: for I am the LORD that healeth thee."

BE PRUDENT

Be discreet, invest in a project, build or buy a house, and have an inheritance that you can leave for your child/children or any relative.

No matter how little the inheritance is, little inheritance is better than no inheritance.

Be remembered for the good you did and the things that you left for your family and friends.

You cannot do any capital project without preparing for it and being mindful of your expenses.

Prioritize your expenses and do without some wants so that you can have enough money to do something that will be your legacy.

Think and start working on something that you will leave for your children, friends, or family.

If you don't start now, you may never start.

If you don't have enough money to start a capital project right now, begin to study about it, prepare for it and save toward it.

The Lord will help you to make it happen. Amen.

Proverbs 13:22 "A good man leaveth an inheritance to his children's children: And the wealth of the sinner is laid up for the just."

Proverbs 19:14 "House and riches are the inheritance of fathers: And a prudent wife is from the LORD."

NEVER TAKE ANYTHING AT FACE VALUE

Examine everything and anyone you may have dealings with, especially business dealings.

The Gibeonites deceived Joshua and the Israelites for their selfish reason (Joshua 9:3-27).

Someone else wants what you have and may want to rob you of what you have deceitfully.

Listen attentively, look for tell-tale signs, inquire from others, and look people in the eyes when you discuss.

Don't be rushed to do or invest in anything. Take your time!

Taking your time makes you ask questions and see what was previously oblivious to you.

Say no to any proposal that you are not convinced about.

Don't let anyone fool you that you will understand it by and by.

Let no one downplay your concerns or questions.

If something matters to you, it should be looked into and resolved before you enter into any business dealings or purchase anything.

Think about it, watch, and pray.

Most importantly, commit everything to God and let the Holy Spirit reveal the hearts and minds of men to you.

God is able to show you the ending of a thing from the beginning, thereby making you know how anything will end before it starts.

This is a great benefit to believers.

You need to ask God to show you what you cannot see in any transaction.

1 Thessalonians 5:21 "But examine everything carefully; hold fast to that which is good;" NASB1995

Psalm 37:5 "Commit thy way unto the LORD; Trust also in him; And he shall bring it to pass."

Hebrews 4:12-13 "For the word of God is alive and powerful. It is sharper than the sharpest two-edged sword, cutting between soul and spirit, between joint and marrow. It exposes our innermost thoughts and desires. Nothing in all creation is hidden from God. Everything is naked and exposed before his eyes, and he is the one to whom we are accountable." NLT

BE MERCIFUL TO OTHERS

You will receive mercy if you are merciful to others.

Jesus forgave you your sins and blotted them out with His blood.

Do likewise by forgiving others.

Forgiving people does not mean that you excuse them for their bad behavior or you allow them to do the same bad behavior to you again.

It means not speaking ill of them or doing the bad they have done against you against them.

Jesus does not want you to repay evil with evil because it doesn't exemplify the nature of God.

You are a child of God if you exemplify the nature of God.

Forgiving others make others see God in you and be attracted to the God in you.

Forgiving others makes you effective in the ministry of reconciliation that God has given to you as a believer.

If you don't forgive others, God will not forgive you your sins.

It's not easy to forgive those who have hurt you.

Pray to God to help you to be merciful to others and to forgive those who have hurt you.

Receive God's help and grace to be merciful and to forgive those who have hurt you.

Luke 6:36 "Be ye therefore merciful, as your Father also is merciful."

Matthew 5:16 "Let your light so shine before men, that they may see your good works, and glorify your Father which is in heaven."

Ephesians 4:32 "and be ye kind one to another, tenderhearted, forgiving one another, even as God for Christ's sake hath forgiven you."

Matthew 18:32-34 "Then his Lord, after that he had called him, said unto him, O thou wicked servant, I forgave thee all that debt because thou desiredst me: shouldest not thou also have had compassion on thy fellow-servant, even as I had pity on thee? And his Lord was wroth, and delivered him to the tormentors, till he should pay all that was due unto him."

Matthew 6:14 "If you forgive those who sin against you, your heavenly Father will forgive you." NLT

ENJOY WHO YOU ARE AND WHAT YOU HAVE RIGHT NOW

The secret of a rich life is enjoying your life every day.

Fulfillment comes from God and not from who you are or what you have.

Jesus has come to give you a free and abundant life.

The Holy Spirit told me that any day that I did not enjoy will never come back.

Therefore, I made a decision to enjoy each day, no matter how challenging it is.

This disposition makes me not be overwhelmed, stressed, or unhappy.

Jesus came to destroy the works of the devil so that you can live a victorious and enjoyable life.

Jesus said that in this world, you would have tribulations, but be of good cheer, be happy, expectant, and hopeful of what God will do each day of your life because Jesus has overcome the world.

Believe that God loads you daily with benefits.

Tell yourself always that you can do all things through Christ who strengthens you.

Don't look back and wish you enjoyed your life while going through a situation that does not exist anymore.

Remind yourself always that this difficult situation shall pass.

Surround yourself with friends who know and believe the Word of God. Friends who encourage you by the Holy Scriptures and the Holy Spirit.

Stay away from people who discourage you and make you unhappy.

Believe that God will provide for your needs.

Pray for the wisdom to know how to enjoy your life with what you have.

You don't have to go on vacation to enjoy life.

Worshipping God and being in the presence of God give you fullness of joy and pleasure forevermore.

Find out who you are and what makes you happy. You will make yourself happy by knowing and doing what you enjoy.

Dressing up makes me happy.

Don't depend on others to make you happy. Your happiness will fluctuate according to their moods.

Only God is constant in a changing world. Look to Him at all times, and you will be happy and not ashamed.

1 Samuel 23:15–16 "One day near Horesh, David received the news that Saul was on the way to Ziph to search for him and kill him. Jonathan went to find David and encouraged him to stay strong in his faith in God. "Don't be afraid," Jonathan reassured him. "My father will never find you! You are going to be the king of Israel, and I will be next to you, as my father, Saul, is well aware."" NLT

Psalm 34:4–5 "I asked the Lord for help, and he answered me. He saved me from all that I feared. Those who go to him for help are happy. They are never disgraced." ICB

Psalms 16:11 "Thou wilt shew me the path of life: in thy presence is fulness of joy; at thy right hand, there are pleasures for evermore."

John 10:10 "The thief comes only in order to steal and kill and destroy. I came that they may have *and* enjoy life and have it in abundance (to the full, till it overflows)." AMPC

GO THE EXTRA MILE

Always do more than is expected of you, except for things that require authorization from a superior.

Only fools promote without testing.

God and man will promote you after you have been proven.

Be passionate about all that you do.

Choose what you agree to do and do all that you do carefully and with wisdom.

Don't do too much that you're not able to do all things excellently.

Doing things excellently will make you be preferred above others.

You are fully responsible for whatever you have agreed to do; therefore, think carefully and count the cost before you say yes to any assignment.

Courteously reject an assignment that you know God does not want you to do and that you don't have the time to do.

You can't please everyone and please God at the same time.

Also, know that you matter; therefore, let others respect your decision.

If anyone is not happy with your decision, pray about it and let God work on his/her heart.

It's better to please God than man. Do not take any assignment, give your money toward or do anything because of fear or compulsion.

Do not be part of anything that is not in line with God's Word and God's will for your life.

Don't take an assignment that you don't have the grace, time, conviction, gift, and resources to do.

Acts 5:29 "Then Peter and the other apostles answered and said, We ought to obey God rather than men."

Daniel 6:3 "Then this Daniel was preferred above the presidents and princes because an excellent spirit was in him; and the king thought to set him over the whole realm."

2 Corinthians 9:7 "Each of you should give what you have decided in your heart to give, not reluctantly or under compulsion, for God loves a cheerful giver." GW

EAT WELL, REST WELL AND EXERCISE

You will live in the same body all the days of your life.

You need a healthy body to partner with God to fulfill God's purpose on earth.

Be committed to eating a healthy balanced diet and maintaining a balanced body weight.

Determine an age, genetic, gender and height appropriate body weight and maintain that body weight through controlled eating and exercise.

The Bible says bodily exercise profits little (1 Timothy 4:8a), thereby attesting to the benefits of exercise.

Furthermore, rest well by having a structured life that helps you live a stress free or a stress managed life. Prioritize what you do and delegate what you are not able to do.

You can't do everything. Don't wear yourself out by doing more than you are capable of doing.

Stress is the root cause of many diseases. Don't let people's expectations wear you out.

God will not put too much on you than you can bear. If you are stressed out, pray and ask God for help and the wisdom to know what you have to do, what you have to delegate, and what you have to give up.

God will always hear your prayers and give you the wisdom and the help you need to overcome every distressed or challenging situation.

God will always send the help you need to accomplish His will and purpose.

Also, inquire from close people who do what you do, how they do all that they do.

You may gain wisdom from how they do all that they do without being stressed out.

God understands your frailty, human limitations, and frustrations. That is why God was not angry with Moses when he complained about being overwhelmed and stressed.

God will not tell you to do anything that He has not given you the grace to do.

Exodus 18:13, 17-18, 21-22 "And it came to pass on the morrow, that Moses sat to judge the people: and the people stood by Moses from the morning unto the evening. And Moses' father in law said unto him, The thing that thou doest is not good. Thou wilt surely wear away, both thou and this people that is with thee: for this thing is too heavy for thee; thou art not able to perform it thyself alone. Moreover, thou shalt provide out of all the people able men, such as fear God, men of truth, hating covetousness; and place such over them, to be rulers of thousands, and rulers of hundreds, rulers of fifties, and rulers of tens: and let them judge the people at all seasons: and it shall be, that every great matter they shall bring unto thee, but every small matter they shall judge: so shall it be easier for thyself, and they shall bear the burden with thee."

Numbers 11:14 "I am not able to bear all this people alone, because it is too heavy for me."

Psalm 61:1–2 "O God, listen to my cry! Hear my prayer! From the ends of the earth, I cry to you for help when my heart is overwhelmed."

1 Corinthians 10:13 "There hath no temptation taken you but such as is common to man: but God is faithful, who will not suffer you to be tempted above that ye are able; but will with the temptation also make a way to escape, that ye may be able to bear it."

Numbers 11:11, 16-17 "And Moses said unto the LORD, Wherefore hast thou afflicted thy servant? and wherefore have I not found favour in thy sight, that thou layest the burden of all this people upon me? And the LORD said unto Moses, Gather unto me seventy men of the elders of Israel, whom thou knowest to be the elders of the people and officers over them; and bring them unto the tabernacle of the congregation, that they may stand there with thee. And I will come down and talk with thee there: and I will take of the spirit which is upon thee, and will put it upon them; and they shall bear the burden of the people with thee, that thou bear it not thyself alone."

LIVE A LIFE OF IMPACT

Your life is measured and relevant according to your impact and purpose.

God is a God of purpose, and He has a purpose for your existence.

You are alive because God still has a purpose for your life.

Discover God's purpose for your life through prayers, the leading of the Holy Spirit, and by paying close attention to your talent and gift. You were born for a purpose.

Be passionate about discovering and fulfilling it.

Block out distractions by being focused on your purpose through preparation and total commitment to your purpose, and the things that matter to your purpose.

Be fully trained by God through the teaching and guidance of the Holy Spirit and by man through training, impartation and experience.

Spend time becoming who God wants you to be.

You have to be intentional about fulfilling your purpose.

Every day of your life must be lived purposefully. Don't live carelessly and aimlessly.

Live to be an instrument of blessing each and every day of your life, for this is the reason for your purpose.

Don't just fulfill your purpose; believe God to finish your purpose before you die.

Jeremiah 29:11 ""For I know the plans I have for you," declares the Lord, "plans to prosper you and not to harm you, plans to give you hope and a future."" NIV

John 4:34 "Jesus said to them, My food (nourishment) is to do the will (pleasure) of Him Who sent Me and to accomplish and completely finish His work." AMPC

2 Timothy 4:6-7 "For I am now ready to be offered, and the time of my departure is at hand. I have fought a good fight, I have finished my course, I have kept the faith." AMPC

John 18:37 "Pilate therefore said unto him, Art thou a king then? Jesus answered, Thou sayest that I am a king. To this end was I born, and for this cause came I into the world, that I should bear witness unto the truth. Every one that is of the truth heareth my voice."

LOVE EVERYONE

God revealed His mind that He loves everyone in John 3:16.

Don't judge people; love them by praying for them.

Speak the truth in love. Do all things through love.

Don't just pray for people; give to them whatever you can. The proof of love is giving. For God so loved the world, that He gave His only begotten Son.

God loved us so much that Christ died for our sins when we were sinners.

Don't love only people who are educated, accomplished, and look like you; love people who are not privileged like you and can't give you anything. Don't despise anyone's little beginnings.

Love people who are sick by praying for their healing and by comforting them in any way you can.

Love those who are addicted by praying for their deliverance.

Love those are are living without Christ by praying for their salvation, by preaching Christ to them, and by being an example of a believer to them.

Love those who are living aimlessly by supporting them to find their purpose in life and by impacting their lives.

Love the poor enough to pray for their provision and by giving to them.

Show the love of Christ through your love, intercession, compassion, sincerity, and giving.

Love with discernment and knowledge. Don't partake in people's sins because you love them. Don't allow people to abuse you because you love them.

The love of God is already shared in your heart by the Holy Spirit, and the Holy Spirit will enable you to love others.

Importantly, you can't love others if you don't love yourself. Jesus said that you should love others as you love yourself.

Matthew 22:39 "The second most important commandment is like this one. And it is, "Love others as much as you love yourself."" CEV

Romans 5:8 "But God commendeth his love toward us, in that, while we were yet sinners, Christ died for us."

Ephesians 4:15 "but speaking the truth in love, may grow up into him in all things, which is the head, even Christ."

1 Corinthians 16:14 "And do everything with love." NLT

Philippians 1:9-10 "And this I pray, that your love may abound yet more and more in knowledge and in all judgment; that ye may approve things that are excellent; that ye may be sincere and without offence till the day of Christ."

BE PATIENT

Patience is a fruit of the Holy Spirit, and it's required in your walk with God, to receive from God and in your relationship with others.

God has precious promises for you in the Bible, and He might have given you specific vision(s) and promise(s).

No matter how long the fulfillment of the vision and promise take, wait patiently on and for the Lord.

Abraham continued to believe in God for the fulfillment of Isaac's birth when it seemed the promise might not be fulfilled anymore. Abraham never lost hope in the faithfulness of God to fulfill His promise.

Don't lose hope in God. Don't give up on the vision and promises of God for you.

Though it delays, according to your estimation, it will surely come to pass.

God is not a man that He should lie. He is able to do what He has promised to do for you.

Acquaint yourself with God and wait patiently for God's timing.

Encourage yourself through the comfort of the Holy Spirit, Scriptures and by singing praises to God.

Inquire from God about what you need to do while you wait for the fulfillment of His vision and promise to you.

Take your eyes off the vision and put your eyes on God.

Waiting patiently for the fulfillment of a vision or promise matures and prepares you to be ready to do what God has called you to do.

This is why God makes you wait patiently to receive from Him.

Do not worry about what God has in His control.

Acts 1:6-7 "While the apostles were still with Jesus, they asked him, "Lord, are you now going to give Israel its own king again?" Jesus said to them, "You don't need to know the time of those events that only the Father controls."" CEV

Romans 5:3-4 "And not only so, but we glory in tribulations also: knowing that tribulation worketh patience; and patience, experience; and experience, hope."

Romans 4:17-21 "(as it is written, I have made thee a father of many nations) before him whom he believed, even God, who quickeneth the dead, and calleth those things which be not as though they were. Who against hope believed in hope, that he might become the father of many nations, according to that which was spoken, So shall thy seed be. And being not weak in faith, he considered not his own body now dead, when he was about an hundred years old, neither yet the deadness of Sarah's womb: he staggered not at the promise of God through unbelief; but was strong in faith, giving glory to God; and being fully persuaded that, what he had promised, he was able also to perform."

Habakkuk 2:3 "The vision will still happen at the appointed time. It hurries toward its goal. It won't be a lie. If it's delayed, wait for it. It will certainly happen. It won't be late." GW

BE PEACEABLE

As much as you can, live peaceably with everyone.

Let go of your pride and of always trying to be right. Unity cannot be achieved without peace.

You don't have to agree with others to be peaceable. You can live in peace with those who do not have the same beliefs, background, and lifestyle as yours.

Being peaceable with others starts by knowing that you can't change anyone. It is accepting others for who they are and believing that God will change their perspective or lifestyle if they are wrong.

Instead of arguing and fighting for your right or belief, take a moment to pray for God's will to be made known and done in the lives of the people that are involved in the argument.

When God's will is made known and done, all arguments will cease.

Also, let God fight for Himself and unveil His mind and will to others. It took you some time to know God and have the knowledge of God.

Therefore, give people time to grow in their relationship with God and in the knowledge of God.

Always remind yourself that God commands His blessing in unity, and this should be your desire and goal more than winning an argument.

Don't agree with anything or anyone who is against the Holy Scriptures but live in peace so that you can exemplify the nature of Christ and win souls for Christ.

Romans 12:18 "As much as it is possible, live in peace with everyone." GW

1 Corinthians 9:19-23 "Even though I am a free man with no master, I have become a slave to all people to bring many to Christ. When I was with the Jews, I lived like a Jew to bring the Jews to Christ. When I was with those who follow the Jewish law. I, too, lived under that law. Even though I am not subject to the law, I did this so I could bring to Christ those who are under the law. When I am with the Gentiles, who do not follow the Jewish law, I, too, live apart from that law so I can bring them to Christ. But I do not ignore the law of God; I obey the law of Christ. When I am with those who are weak, I share their weakness, for I want to bring the weak to Christ. Yes, I try to find common ground with everyone, doing everything I can to save some. I do everything to spread the Good News and share in its blessings." NLT

NOTHING COMES OR GETS DONE BY WISHING

If wishes were horses, beggars would ride. Don't be lazy. Get up and work toward your goal.

God will empower you to work and fulfill your purpose, but you have to work to fulfill your purpose.

Learn to manage your time effectively and be accountable to yourself or someone, if needed.

Break down your goals into achievable parts and work on a part per time so that you will not be overwhelmed.

Make sure that your goal is measurable and achievable and have an estimated timeline for fulfilling each part of the goal.

Don't just pray. work, too. Faith without works is dead. Pray and work toward your dream and purpose in life.

Know that you are partner with God in the fulfillment of His purpose and plan for your life. There is the part that God will do, and there is the part you have to do.

Be sensitive to the leading of the Holy Spirit and be willing to do what the Holy Spirit tells you to do.

Acts 13:2-5, 14, 49 "As they ministered to the Lord, and fasted, the Holy Ghost said, Separate me Barnabas and Saul for the work whereunto I have called them. And when they had fasted and prayed and laid their hands on them, they sent them away. So they, being sent forth by the Holy Ghost, departed unto Seleucia, and from thence, they sailed to Cyprus. And when they were at Salamis, they preached the word of God in the synagogues of the Jews: and they had also John to their minister. But when they departed from Perga, they came to Antioch in Pisidia and went into the synagogue on the sabbath day, and sat down. And the word of the Lord was published throughout all the region."

Proverbs 6:9-11 "How long will you lie there, you lazy bum? When will you get up from your sleep? "Just a little sleep, just a little slumber, just a little nap. Then your poverty will come ⌐ to you ⌐ like a drifter, and your need will come ⌐ to you ⌐ like a bandit."" GW

1 Corinthians 15:10 "But whatever I am now, it is all because God poured out his special favor on me—and not without results. For I have worked harder than any of the other apostles, yet it was not I but God who was working through me by his grace." NLT

YOU NEED HELP

You cannot do anything and everything by your power.

There are unseen evil forces and adversaries that work against you, the fulfillment of your purpose, and your success. You need the supernatural help of God to overcome the attacks of the enemy.

Ask God for His help always. My constant prayer is: "God help me." Start each day by asking God for His help through prayer.

Let God know that you need His presence, His strength, His help, and His grace to do all that you have to do.

God knows that without Him, you can do nothing, but He still wants you to pray to Him for help.

Prayer is much more than asking God for help. Prayer is an act of entering into the presence of God to commune with God.

Prayer is about communication with God. It is about having a personal relationship with the Father.

Prayer is talking to God and hearing from God. You may not hear God at first, but with faith and by being quiet in God's presence, you will begin to feel and hear God speaking to your heart.

Prayer is access to God. Prayer grants you access to God by the blood of Jesus and the opportunity to present your requests to God.

Prayer allows you to worship and praise the Lord, thereby receiving His strength and help.

Prayer also allows you to offer confession of your sins, which leads to genuine repentance.

Prayer strengthens you and enables you to do God's will.

All aspects of prayer involve communication with God through Jesus Christ with the help of the Holy Spirit.

God wants you to have a personal relationship with Him, and He wants to commune with you through prayer. Welcome God into your life by accepting Jesus Christ as your Lord and Savior.

Matthew 7:7-8 "Ask, and it shall be given you; seek, and ye shall find; knock, and it shall be opened unto you: for everyone that asketh receiveth; and he that seeketh findeth; and to him that knocketh it shall be opened."

2 Chronicles 20:22 "And when they began to sing and to praise, the LORD set ambushments against the children of Ammon, Moab, and mount Seir, which were come against Judah; and they were smitten."

Genesis 49:23-25 "With bitterness, archers attacked him; they shot at him with hostility. But his bow remained steady, his strong arms stayed limber, because of the hand of the Mighty One of Jacob, because of the Shepherd, the Rock of Israel, because of your father's God, who helps you, because of the Almighty, who blesses you with blessings of the skies above, blessings of the deep springs below, blessings of the breast and womb." NIV

1 Chronicles 16:11 "Seek the Lord and His strength; yearn for and seek His face and to be in His presence continually!" AMPC

DISCERN YOUR APPOINTED TIME BY THE SPIRIT OF GOD

Step into the atmosphere and timing that God has prepared for you by faith and trust in God.

Believe that God has given you all you need when He places you to function in any capacity.

Don't let fear hold you back from stepping into the higher dimension of greatness that God has called you to attain. You can be who God wants you to be, and you can have what God wants you to have.

David seized the moment when he volunteered to fight Goliath while on an errand to give food to his brothers at the war front.

By seizing the moment, he was publicly announced to King Saul and the entire Israelites.

This was the beginning of his readiness and acceptance by the people of Israel to become the king of Israel and to step into the moment and kingship that he was destined for.

Do not miss your moment and time to be who God has destined you to be. Perceive your moment and seize your moment!

It's your time to arise, shine and do what you were destined to do!

1 Samuel 17:17-18, 20, 32, 37, 46, 48-49 "And Jesse said unto David his son, Take now for thy brethren an ephah of this parched corn, and these ten loaves, and run to the camp to thy brethren; and carry these ten cheeses unto the captain of their thousand, and look how thy brethren fare, and take their pledge. And David rose up early in the morning, and left the sheep with a keeper, and took, and went, as Jesse had commanded him; and he came to the trench, as the host was going forth to the fight, and shouted for the battle. And David said to Saul, Let no man's heart fail because of him; thy servant will go and fight with this Philistine. David said moreover, The LORD that delivered me out of the paw of the lion, and out of the paw of the bear, he will deliver me out of the hand of this Philistine. And Saul said unto David, Go, and the LORD be with thee. This day will the LORD deliver thee into mine hand; and I will smite thee, and take thine head from thee; and I will give the carcases of the host of the Philistines this day unto the fowls of the air, and to the wild beasts of the earth; that all the earth may know that there is a God in Israel. And it came to pass, when the Philistine arose, and came and drew nigh to meet David, that David hasted, and ran toward the army to meet the Philistine. And David put his hand in his bag, and took thence a stone, and slang it, and smote the Philistine in his forehead, that the stone sunk into his forehead; and he fell upon his face to the earth."

2 Samuel 5:12 "And David perceived that the LORD had established him king over Israel and that he had exalted his kingdom for his people Israel's sake."

2 Samuel 5:1-3 "Then came all the tribes of Israel to David unto Hebron, and spake, saying, Behold, we are thy bone and thy flesh. Also in time past, when Saul was king over us, thou wast he that leddest out and broughtest in Israel: and the LORD said to thee, Thou shalt feed my people Israel, and thou shalt be a captain over Israel. So all the elders of Israel came to the king to Hebron; and king David made a league with them in Hebron before the LORD: and they anointed David king over Israel."

BE HUMBLE

Do not be proud or ashamed to seek help from others. An increase in your family, business, and ministry requires people to work with you. Pray for faithful men and women to support you in what you are doing.

Asking for any kind of help is not something to be ashamed of. As long as you live, you will need people to help you to be able to function and be successful in what God has called you to do.

Your vision and business will be very small if you don't need help or you don't want to ask for help. The greater you are, the more needy you become.

Don't despise or maltreat those who God has brought to help you. They have been given to you by God to work with you so that you can fulfill God's purpose for your life. Pray for them. Cherish them.

Use the money that people have donated to support you or invest in your business wisely and according to the plan or your contract/agreement.

Encourage your workers. Train them to be experienced and more suitable for the job.

Do not despise your workers. You don't know what God has in store for them.

Pay your workers on time. Seek their good and show them that you care.

The success and longevity of your business depend on God and the workers who represent you. Let your workers be proud to work for you and represent you.

Be a good example of a believer to your workers so that they will come to Christ through you.

Be humble, Jesus is humble, and God hates the proud.

Luke 5:5-7 ""Master", Simon replied, "we worked hard all last night and didn't catch a thing. But if you say so, I'll let the nets down again." And this time, their nets were so full of fish they began to tear! A shout for help brought their partners in the other boat, and soon both boats were filled with fish and on the verge of sinking." NLT

Deuteronomy 24:14-15 "Thou shalt not oppress an hired servant that is poor and needy, whether he be of thy brethren, or of thy strangers that are in thy land within thy gates: at his day thou shalt give him his hire, neither shall the sun go down upon it; for he is poor, and setteth his heart upon it: lest he cry against thee unto the LORD, and it be sin unto thee."

YOU NEED FAVOR! YOU CAN'T EXCEL WITHOUT FAVOR

You can't be preferred above others without favor. You can't be accepted by others without favor. You can't be supported by others without favor.

You need the favor of God and others to achieve greatness. Jesus and Samuel needed the favor of God and man for the establishment of their ministries and greatness.

Pray for favor. Be a person of integrity so that you can be trusted and favored. Do not abuse the favor that has been given to you.

Be grateful to God and man for the favor that you have received. Maintain and value your relationship with God and man so that you can continually be favored.

Continue to do good and be consistent in what bring favor to your life.

You can lose the presence and favor of God and man. Pray and desist from behaviors that may cause disfavor.

Without favor, you can't go far in life, and you can't be who God wants you to be and have all that God wants you to have.

Without favor, life will be hard for you. Be humble and receive the favor of God and man.

Luke 2:52 "And Jesus increased in wisdom and stature and in favour with God and man."

1 Samuel 2:26 "And the child Samuel grew on and was in favour both with the LORD and also with men."

VALUE AND PROTECT YOUR RELATIONSHIPS WITH OTHERS

If someone gives you access to his/her family, ministry, business, or friends, never abuse it. A protocol is required for decorum.

Don't ever disclose situations or things in someone's home, ministry, or career that you were privy to.

You will reap what you sow. If you sow the seed of covering others' secrets, you will reap the harvest of the covering of your own secrets.

If you give someone access to your mind, be mindful and careful of what you tell them. Once a word is said, you have lost control of what the hearer will do with the word. Don't be careless!

Don't go above those who gave you access or an opportunity to soar and fulfill your dreams. Consult them and ask for their permission and approval.

Don't use and dump people. Don't be desperate! Let God have His way in your life. Let God connect you to the right people at the right time in His own way.

Let God open doors for you, and nobody will be a god in your life. Don't live in fear of man and be ensnared because you looked to man and not God for greatness.

If you look to God, you will not be ashamed. Don't put any man in the place that is meant for God. If you do this, you will be disappointed and frustrated.

Pray for and stand by the people who gave you access and a platform to be great. Speak well of them and honor them as much as you can. Don't bite the hand that fed you.

Celebrate access to God and man because access is costly. Our access to God costs Jesus His life. Your access to man will cost his/her privacy and reputation.

Respect access and you will have more access, open doors, and opportunities to be blessed and be all that God wants you to be.

Proverbs 11:13 "A talebearer revealeth secrets: but he that is of a faithful spirit concealeth the matter."

Hebrews 10:19-20 "Therefore, believers, since we have confidence and full freedom to enter the Holy Place [the place where God dwells] by [means of] the blood of Jesus, by this new and living way which He initiated and opened for us through the veil [as in the Holy of Holies], that is, through His flesh." AMP

Galatians 1:18 "Then after three years I went up to Jerusalem to see Peter, and abode with him fifteen days."

Acts 9:26-27 "And when Saul was come to Jerusalem, he assayed to join himself to the disciples: but they were all afraid of him, and believed not that he was a disciple. But

Barnabas took him and brought him to the apostles, and declared unto them how he had seen the Lord in the way, and that he had spoken to him, and how he had preached boldly at Damascus in the name of Jesus."

BE FLEXIBLE

Be willing and ready to start life all over again if this is the route God is leading you.

God sometimes takes away the first to establish a new covenant or beginning.

Don't be rigid, be flexible to the leading of God through the Holy Spirit.

Trust God's plan and follow God's plan for your life. Your success is in your obedience to God and His will for you. Think about this: "What if Abraham had stayed in Haran when God told him to leave?" Abraham would have continued to worship the idols of his father, Terah, and not have a deep relationship with God.

Abraham would not have received the covenant and promise. Abraham would not have become the father of many nations, and the Gentiles would not have received the blessing of Abraham through faith in Jesus Christ.

There might have been no Israel, and Abraham might not have been known by anyone who is living at this time. Also, Abraham would not have been called the friend of God because Jesus said, " if you obey Him out of love, His Father will love you, and He and His Father will abide with you." (John 14:21).

Or God would have fulfilled the purpose He had for Abraham through someone else, because God's plan, purpose, will and counsel must surely come to pass (Isaiah 46:10).

Please don't let God have to replace you. Don't watch someone else fulfill God's revealed will, purpose and plan for your life.

It's painful and heartbreaking to watch someone else do what you know in your heart God meant for you to do.

Obey God and do whatsoever He wants you to do (John 2:5). You will not have to do it alone. He will actually do it through you. God will be there with you as you start life all over, if this is His will for you and your family.

Starting life all over could be stressful, but you will be helped and blessed by God if this is God's will for you.

Be where God wants you to be at all times, and you will see that God's grace will be more than sufficient for you.

Go with God; you can never be wrong or disappointed doing so. Don't consider your age or anything; consider God's Word and God's integrity.

Genesis 12:1-5 "Now the LORD had said unto Abram, Get thee out of thy country, and from thy kindred, and from thy father's house, unto a land that I will shew thee: and I will make of thee a great nation, and I will bless thee, and make thy name great, and thou shalt be a blessing: and I will bless them that bless thee, and curse him that curseth thee: and in thee shall all families of the earth be blessed. So Abram departed, as the LORD had spoken unto him; and Lot went with him: and Abram was seventy and five years old when he departed out of Haran. And Abram took Sarai his wife, and Lot his brother's son, and all their substance that they had gathered, and the souls that they had gotten in Haran; and they went forth to go into the land of Canaan, and into the land of Canaan they came."

Isaiah 51:2 "Look unto Abraham, your father, and unto Sarah that bare you: for I called him alone, and blessed him, and increased him."

Genesis 17:1-2 "And when Abram was ninety years old and nine, the LORD appeared to Abram, and said unto him, I am the Almighty God; walk before me and be thou perfect. And I will make my covenant between me and thee and will multiply thee exceedingly."

Galatians 3:13-14 "Christ hath redeemed us from the curse of the law, being made a curse for us: for it is written, Cursed is everyone that hangeth on a tree: that the blessing of Abraham might come on the Gentiles through Jesus Christ; that we might receive the promise of the Spirit through faith."

DON'T COMPARE YOURSELF WITH OTHERS

You are unique, and the path that God takes you is different from others.

Everything you go through makes you who God wants you to be. God even works your mistakes together for His good.

Believe God's will and way for you is the best for you.

Accept that the people God has planted in your life are suitable and perfect for the performance of God's will and purpose for your life.

If the grass is greener on the other side, it's because the grass was watered.

Celebrate yourself and invest in yourself. Be grateful to God for the people who are in your life and make them better so that they can be blessed to be a blessing to you.

Don't compare yourselves with people who tell you half-truths, and you don't know the source of their blessings.

Don't compare yourselves with people who are gifted to do something that is different from what you are gifted to do. There is something that nobody does like you, and you are better at doing than everyone else.

Comparing yourself with others brings covetousness, and God is against covetousness.

Comparing yourself with others makes you ungrateful, and God is against an ungrateful spirit.

Comparing yourself with others is questioning the wisdom and sovereignty of God.

Comparing yourself with others breaks your focus, and it brings distractions that take you out of God's plan and purpose for your life.

Comparing yourself with others brings envy and jealousy. Comparing yourself with others makes you unhappy, and it drains your ingenuity and energy.

It can lead to sin and spiritual death. Do not compare yourself with anyone because there is none like you among all the creations of God.

You were created the way you are for a purpose, and you are gifted uniquely to fulfill that purpose.

Rejoice with others and believe God that great things will happen in your life that will make others rejoice with you, too.

Believe God has been good to you in all things, and rejoice in all that God has freely given you to have and to enjoy.

When you are faithful over a few things and grateful in all things, God will place you over more things.

Psalm 73:1-3, 16-19 "Truly God is good to Israel, Even to such as are of a clean heart. But as for me, my feet were almost gone; My steps had well nigh slipped, For I was envious at the foolish When I saw the prosperity of the wicked. When I thought to know this, It was too painful for me; Until I went into the sanctuary of God; Then understood I their end. Surely thou didst set them in slippery places: Thou castedst them down into destruction. How are they brought into desolation, as in a moment! They are utterly consumed with terrors."

2 Corinthians 10:12 "Oh, don't worry; we wouldn't dare say that we are as wonderful as these other men who tell you how important they are! But they are only comparing themselves with each other, using themselves as the standard of measurement. How ignorant!" NLT

Exodus 20:17 "You must not covet your neighbor's house. You must not covet your neighbor's wife, male or female servant, ox or donkey, or anything else that belongs to your neighbor." NLT

Romans 8:28 "And we know that God causes everything to work together for the good of those who love God and are called according to his purpose for them." NLT

EMPOWER YOUR IMMEDIATE FAMILY

Invest all that you are and all that you have in your immediate family.

Your seed will continue to live when you are dead. You continue to live through your seed.

As much as you can, do not let your seed and generation be substandard after your lifetime.

Do your part in empowering your children to be who God wants them to be. Be consistently committed to your children spiritually, physically, emotionally, academically and financially.

Take full responsibility for the well-being of your children, even when you pay people to cater to their needs. Whatever negative thing that happens to your children affects you more than anyone.

Don't be careless with the upbringing of your children. Be fully involved. Supervise, monitor, and correct those that have access to your children.

Review what your children are being taught to ensure that they are taught according to God's Word.

Correct your children. Discipline them when they come short of the required standard. Study each child to know the most effective discipline. Correction is proof of loving your children.

Don't condone bad attitudes and behaviors. Teach them everything about life. Let your children learn about life from you, so you can be sure that they are taught correctly.

Let your children be free to ask you any questions. Be approachable to your family at all times.

Train your children early so they can conform to God's standards and have a solid foundation that is unmovable. If they desist from God's Word later in life, they have the truth of God's Word that will bring conviction and restoration.

Let your job, ministry, and business revolve around your children. You will have lots of time when they are in college or after they have left home to do some things you are unable to do right now.

Be wise in watching and praying over your children so that the enemy does not corrupt the holy seeds whom God has given you.

Believe God to preserve your children by keeping them from all evil.

Proverbs 22:6 "Train up a child in the way he should go: And when he is old, he will not depart from it."

Proverbs 29:15 "The rod and reproof give wisdom: But a child left to himself bringeth his mother to shame."

Proverbs 3:11-12 "My son, despise not the chastening of the LORD; Neither be weary of his correction: For whom the LORD loveth he correcteth; Even as a father the son in whom he delighteth."

BE READY TO LEARN NEW SKILLS AS YOU AGE

Due to technological advancements, the skills you knew before may not be relevant or required anymore.

Also, changes in your family may require you to learn new skills that pay you more income so that you are able to support your family financially.

Also, as you age, your body may not be suited for the job you are doing if your job requires hard labor.

The end of your previous job might be an opportunity for you to learn new skills and make a career change.

Even if you don't need a career change, learn new skills so that you can volunteer and be a blessing to others.

Be flexible and be sensitive to what God will have you do in different seasons of your life.

It's never too late to learn a new skill. Whatever the situation that requires you to change jobs or learn new skills, trust God to lead you and help you.

Don't be bitter or angry; take it as an opportunity to get better. Your attitude will determine your altitude.

Learning new skills enables you to discover your hidden gifting.

God has a way of leading through circumstances. When the brook dried, God led Elijah to the widow woman.

Trust God to take care of you in every season of your life.

Isaiah 46:4 "Even when you're old, I'll take care of you. Even when your hair turns gray, I'll support you. I made you and will continue to care for you. I'll support you and save you." GW

Psalms 32:8 "The Lord says, ⌐ "I will instruct you. I will teach you the way that you should go. I will advise you as my eyes watch over you."" GW

1 Kings 17:5-9 "So Elijah did as the Lord told him and camped beside Kerith Brook, east of the Jordan. The ravens brought him bread and meat each morning and evening, and he drank from the brook. But after a while, the brook dried up, for there was no rainfall anywhere in the land. Then the Lord said to Elijah, "Go and live in the village of Zarephath, near the city of Sidon. I have instructed a widow there to feed you."" NLT

DON'T BE DISCRIMINATORY

Be open and willing to help whoever God wants you to help.

God created all humans for a purpose. God's purpose is established on the earth and in people's lives when you obey to be channels of blessings.

Let God use you to fulfill His plan and purpose as He wills. If you bless those who look like you and those who can bless you in return, you have received your reward already.

Bless those who God has ordained you to bless. Establish those God has put in your heart to establish. Sponsor the schooling of those who God has brought your way and touched your heart to send to school because their parents cannot afford to send them to school.

Let God count on you to make people be who He has ordained them to be and to have what He has ordained them to have.

Let God answer the prayers of others through you, and He will answer your prayers through other people. Don't choose and pick who to help; let God choose and pick who you should help.

You will be greatly rewarded on earth and in heaven for allowing God to have His will to be done through you.

Acts 10:1-5, 15, 19-20, 28, 34-35, 44-45 "There was a certain man in Cæsarea called Cornelius, a centurion of the band called the Italian band, a devout man, and one that feared God with all his house, which gave much alms to the people and prayed to God always. He saw in a vision evidently about the ninth hour of the day an angel of God coming into him and saying unto him, Cornelius. And when he looked on him, he was afraid and said, What is it, Lord? And he said unto him, Thy prayers and thine alms are come up for a memorial before God. And now send men to Joppa, and call for one Simon, whose surname is Peter: And the voice spake unto him again the second time, What God hath cleansed, that call, not thou common. While Peter thought on the vision, the Spirit said unto him, Behold, three men seek thee. Arise, therefore, and get thee down, and go with them, doubting nothing: for I have sent them. And he said unto them, Ye know how that it is an unlawful thing for a man that is a Jew to keep company or come unto one of another nation; but God hath shewed me that I should not call any man common or unclean. Then Peter opened his mouth, and said, Of a truth I perceive that God is no respecter of persons: but in every nation, he that feareth him, and worketh righteousness, is accepted with him. While Peter yet spake these words, the Holy Ghost fell on all them which heard the word. And they of the circumcision which believed were astonished, as many as came with Peter, because that on the Gentiles also was poured out the gift of the Holy Ghost."

NEVER JUDGE ANYONE

You don't know all the sides of people's issues. Please don't add to their problems by judging and criticizing them.

You can pray and advise others, believing God will take charge of their issues and problems.

Don't judge people by their past or today. Small beginnings do have great tomorrows and endings. See people how God sees them and how He wants you to see them.

Judging people does no good. It makes people feel little and ashamed. Love people enough to pray for them and to stand by them.

Doing these bring healing and comfort to them. It makes you like your Father in heaven, who comforts the afflicted and does not use anyone's past against him/her.

Do not rejoice when evil happens to others. Love takes no pleasure in evil but rejoices over the truth (1 Corinthians 13:6 ICB).

Don't condone other people's sins, but don't judge them either. Speak the truth in love and pray that the truth will set them free.

Judging others makes you unapproachable. You can't preach Christ to others if they are not close to you.

When you judge others, you put yourself on a high pedestal that you may not be able to live up to, thereby setting yourself up to be judged by others and coming short of your own standards or expectations of others.

Be like Apostle Paul, who was all things to all men so that Christ could be preached to all people.

Don't be part of their sins or issues but preach what the Word of God says about what they are going through with love.

Be a shoulder that others can cry on. You are anointed to heal the brokenhearted. Don't add to their bruises or hurts; pray for the healing of their bruises and hurts.

Luke 4:18-19 "The Spirit of the Lord is upon me Because he hath anointed me to preach the gospel to the poor; He hath sent me to heal the brokenhearted, to preach deliverance to the captives, And recovering of sight to the blind, To set at liberty them that are bruised, To preach the acceptable year of the Lord."

Matthew 7:1-5 "Judge not, that ye be not judged. For with what judgment ye judge, ye shall be judged: and with what measure ye mete, it shall be measured to you again. And why beholdest thou the mote that is in thy brother's eye, but considerest not the beam that is in thine own eye? Or how wilt thou say to thy brother, Let me pull out the mote out of thine eye; and, behold, a beam is in thine own eye? Thou hypocrite, first cast out the beam out of thine own eye; and then shalt thou see clearly to cast out the mote out of thy brother's eye."

TAKE CARE OF YOUR FAMILY

Provide for your family. Don't look good at the expense of taking care of your family.

Be mindful of how your family members feel and look. Your children are your reflection more than your designer item.

Sacrifice for the well-being of your family. Be there for your family. Let your family be able to count on you. Have sweet memories with your family that will last you a lifetime.

Look back when you are old, and know that you did your best for your family.

Think about this: "Would you want your children to behave to you in your old age the same way you behaved to them in their childhood?" If your answer is No, please begin to make amends now.

If your children are adults and have left home, seek reconciliation by asking for their forgiveness. With prayers and sincere repentance, the Lord will make your children and family forgive you, restore your relationships, and heal your family.

2 Chronicles 7:14 "Then if my people who are called by my name will humble themselves and pray and seek my face and turn from their wicked ways, I will hear from heaven and will forgive their sins and restore their land." NLT

Genesis 32:19-20 "He also instructed the second, the third, and all the others who followed the herds: "You are to say the same thing to Esau when you meet him. And be sure to say, 'Your servant Jacob is coming behind us.'" For he thought, "I will pacify him with these gifts I am sending on ahead; later, when I see him, perhaps he will receive me."" NIV

Colossians 3:13 "Bear with each other and forgive one another if any of you has a grievance against someone."

FORGIVE AS THE LORD FORGAVE YOU

Never repay good with evil or evil with evil.

My motto is: "I will always remember the good that people did for me, even after doing something upsetting. I will be grateful for the good and continually consider the good."

Our level of relationship may change, but they are still in my good book, and I will always say good things about them based on the good that they did, and do good to them.

Don't expect too much from people so you will not be disappointed. Sometimes, what you perceive as evil that was done to you may be an unreasonable expectation of others and from others.

Even if your good was repaid with evil, the Lord admonishes that you should not repay evil with evil because doing this does not achieve the righteousness and will of God.

Ask God to help you not to repay evil with evil and to forgive those who have repaid your good with evil.

Pray for them that they will receive the wisdom of God and walk in it if they are believers, and the salvation of God, if they are unbelievers.

Let God be glorified through you as you exemplify Christ in all things and at all times.

Do good always so that your prayers can be answered by God and for good things to happen to you.

1 Peter 3:9-12 "Don't repay evil for evil. Don't retaliate with insults when people insult you. Instead, pay them back with a blessing. That is what God has called you to do, and he will grant you his blessing. For the Scriptures say, "If you want to enjoy life and see many happy days, keep your tongue from speaking evil and your lips from telling lies. Turn away from evil and do good. Search for peace, and work to maintain it. The eyes of the Lord watch over those who do right, and his ears are open to their prayers. But the Lord turns his face against those who do evil."" NLT

Matthew 5:16 "Let your light so shine before men, that they may see your good works, and glorify your Father which is in heaven."

YOU DON'T KNOW IT ALL

Learn from God by constantly reading your Bible. Learn from others by reading their books, and listening to their messages and testimonies.

You know more when you learn more. Your life journey becomes easier and richer when you learn from the examples and mistakes of others.

Be humble, and sit at the feet of Jesus so that you can receive instructions and directions from Him.

Jesus is the way, the truth, and the life. He knows the way because He is the way. Seek Him and enquire at all times from Him. Don't be presumptuous, and don't make use of old instructions for present challenges.

Ask God for instructions again and again, and receive fresh instructions from God.

Ask others questions about how they achieved their success, and learn their way of life that is according to God's Word, will, and plan for your life.

Don't copy from others or copy what others are doing. Don't lose your relevance and purpose in life. Use what you have received from others as preparation for God's unique purpose for your life.

Discard what anyone has taught you that is against God's will and purpose for your life, no matter how accomplished the person is.

Deuteronomy 33:3 "Yea, he loved the people; All his saints are in thy hand: And they sat down at thy feet; Everyone shall receive of thy words."

1 Samuel 23:1-5 "Then they told David, saying, Behold, the Philistines fight against Keilah, and they rob the threshingfloors. Therefore David enquired of the LORD, saying, Shall I go and smite these Philistines? And the LORD said unto David, Go, and smite the Philistines, and save Keilah. And David's men said unto him, Behold, we be afraid here in Judah: how much more then if we come to Keilah against the armies of the Philistines? Then David enquired of the LORD yet again. And the LORD answered him and said, Arise, go down to Keilah; for I will deliver the Philistines into thine hand. So David and his men went to Keilah and fought with the Philistines, and brought away their cattle, and smote them with a great slaughter. So David saved the inhabitants of Keilah."

Proverbs 12:15 "Foolish people always do what seems right to them. But wise people listen to advice from others." EASY

DEFINE YOUR RELATIONSHIPS!

Whatever is not defined is vague. Whatever is vague can be misconstrued.

Have boundaries and circles of friendships. A city without walls is a defenseless city that is unprotected (Proverbs 25:28).

Don't make yourself vulnerable. Jesus, during His earthly ministry, had circles of friends and disciples. He had friendships of 1, 3, 12 disciples, larger disciples, and multitudes.

Jesus knew those who believed in Him and those who doubted Him. He knew those to be close to and those to stay away from. He knew the disciples to reveal different levels of revelation.

Ask God to help you to relate with all men according to revelation and their purpose in your life. Know those who God has sent to you and those who God has not sent to you. Do not waste your anointing, time, energy, and resources. Everyone will not believe in you.

Discern and differentiate friendships always. Protect your heart and protect your life. You don't need the whole world to support you and believe in you. You need only people who are connected to your gifting and purpose.

Stop trying to be everybody's friend. Your friend must be someone who you trust will encourage you according to the

Word and will of God for your life. Anyone who does not believe in God's Word and will for your life cannot be your friend.

Differentiate friends from acquaintances. Separate close friends from distant friends and relate with them accordingly.

Choose your friends wisely, and group your friends with wisdom and by their contributions to God's plan and purpose for your life. Review the groupings of your friendships regularly to reflect your state and status in life.

Matthew 17:1-2 "And after six days Jesus taketh Peter, James, and John, his brother, and bringeth them up into an high mountain apart, And was transfigured before them: and his face did shine as the sun, and his raiment was white as the light."

Matthew 10:2–4 "Now the names of the twelve apostles are these; The first, Simon, who is called Peter, and Andrew his brother; James the son of Zebedee, and John his brother; Philip, and Bartholomew; Thomas, and Matthew the publican; James the son of Alphaeus, and Lebbaeus, whose surname was Thaddaeus; Simon the Canaanite, and Judas Iscariot, who also betrayed him."

John 13:23–25 "One of His disciples, whom Jesus loved (esteemed), was leaning against Jesus' chest. So Simon Peter motioned to him (John) and [quietly] asked [him to ask Jesus] of whom He was speaking. Then leaning back against Jesus' chest, he (John) asked Him [privately], "Lord, who is it?"" AMP

Matthew 14:19 "And he commanded the multitude to sit down on the grass, and took the five loaves, and the two fishes, and looking up to heaven, he blessed, and brake, and gave the loaves to his disciples, and the disciples to the multitude."

Luke 10:1 "After this, the Lord appointed 70 other disciples to go ahead of him to every city and place that he intended to go. They were to travel in pairs." GW

BE GRATEFUL!

I am grateful to God for life, for all that I am, and for all that I have. I am what I am by the grace of God. A man can receive nothing except it be given him/her from heaven.

Recognize God's preservation and provision for your life. Worship God! Be grateful to Him for all that He has done for you by loving Him and serving Him with all you are and with all that you have.

Be unapologetic in your worship and praise of God. In God, you live, move, and have your being. Therefore be loyal to God and give Him all that He requires of you by loving Him and serving Him with all your heart, soul, and mind.

Also, be grateful to everyone who God has planted in your life and has contributed to your success and life. You could not have come this far without their prayers and support.

Show gratitude continually to your parents (if both or one of them is still living), your spouse, children, friends, neighbors, colleagues, and anyone who has supported you in any way.

Let them know that their contributions to your life have added momentum to your life and destiny. Appreciate them, honor them, celebrate them, give to them, and be there for them.

Above all, pray for them and preach salvation to any one of them who is unsaved.

You are not self-made. You have received the help of God and man. Every good and perfect gift comes from God. Be grateful to God and be thankful to man!

1 Corinthians 15:10 "But by the grace of God I am what I am: and his grace which was bestowed upon me was not in vain, but I laboured more abundantly than they all: yet not I, but the grace of God which was with me."

Isaiah 25:1, 3-4 "O LORD, thou art my God; I will exalt thee, I will praise thy name; for thou hast done wonderful things; thy counsels of old are faithfulness and truth. Therefore shall the strong people glorify thee, the city of the terrible nations shall fear thee, For thou hast been a strength to the poor, a strength to the needy in his distress, a refuge from the storm, a shadow from the heat when the blast of the terrible ones is as a storm against the wall."

1 Samuel 12:24 "only fear the LORD, and serve him in truth with all your heart: for consider how great things he hath done for you."

Philippians 4:10, 14-16, 18–20 "How I praise the Lord that you are concerned about me again. I know you have always been concerned for me, but you didn't have the chance to help me. Even so, you have done well to share with me in my present difficulty. As you know, you Philippians were the only ones who gave me financial help when I first brought you the Good News and then traveled on from Macedonia. No other church did this. Even when I was in Thessalonica, you sent help more than once. At the moment, I have all I need—and more! I am generously supplied with the gifts you sent me with Epaphroditus. They are a sweet-smelling sacrifice that is acceptable and pleasing to God. And this same God who takes care of me will supply all your needs from his glorious riches, which have been given to us in Christ Jesus. Now all glory to God our Father forever and ever! Amen." NLT

Acts 26:22 "Having therefore obtained help of God, I continue unto this day, witnessing both to small and great, saying none other things than those which the prophets and Moses did say should come."

www.ingramcontent.com/pod-product-compliance
Lightning Source LLC
Chambersburg PA
CBHW051531120626
46551CB00012B/1179